Extreme Steam

Extreme Steam is accompanied by
a fine documentary video programme
of the same name, which is part of
a comprehensive series highlighting
Vanishing World Steam. For full details
of this, and other programmes that
feature Chinese steam in action contact
the publishers at the address below.

Extreme Steam
First published January 2000 by
Tele Rail Publications,
9A New Street,
Carnforth,
Lancs
LA5 9BX

ISBN 0-9537890-0-4

© Tele Rail Publications
No part of this book may be reproduced in any
form without permission from the publishers,
except for the quotation of brief passages for
review.

Printed in the United Kingdom by the
Amadeus Press Ltd, 517 Leeds Road,
Huddersfield, West Yorkshire, HD2 1YJ

Extreme Steam

Compiled by
Steve le Cheminant, Vernon Murphy
Michael Rhodes

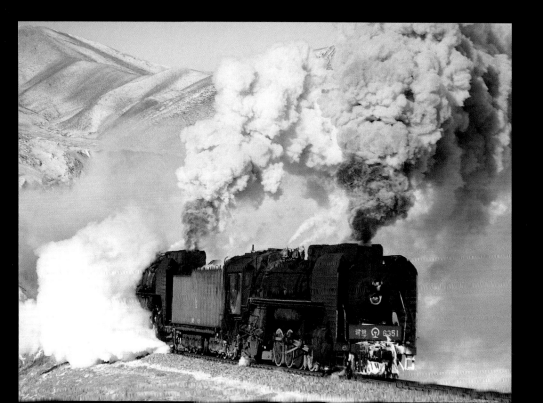

FOR OUR WIVES
Helen, Joan, and Jennifer. Without their patience
and tolerance when we have all had to spend so
much time away from our homes, this book could
never have been completed.

▶

Without the efforts of a handful of dedicated photographers, everyday main line steam scenes like this QJ 2934 making
it's way south near Tongtiantun, on the line from Boli to Linkou, would soon be relegated to just distant memories. *JB*

Contents

Extreme Steam!

Some people might consider our behaviour rather extreme, and I must admit that occasionally we have questioned our own sanity. After all not many people would fly half way around the world, and then spend days on an interminable railway journey, eventually to end up standing around for hours in conditions so extreme that the tiny hairs on the inside of your nose freeze while waiting for a steam train to pass by!

One afternoon had been particularly harsh, and as clouds had rolled in from the north, the midday temperature had fallen to minus 30° centigrade. A freezing 50 kilometres an hour wind was the last straw which had driven all but the terminally insane back to their rooms. Just three of us had remained on the slopes of the Jingpeng pass. Michael survived frostbite free, thanks to a flame red down jacket which has attracted much derision over the years. Vernon Murphy lost part of the covering to his nose and cheeks in a particularly uncomfortable race across an exposed viaduct, and my fingers were numb for weeks as a result of not being able to protect my hands properly as I carried my huge Sony Betacam outfit and tripod.

And yet since that day we've all been drawn back to China time and time again on our now annual pilgrimage. So just how do you define the attraction of China's steam railways? In an age where so many experiences have been reduced to a packaged parody of real life in some theme park or other – this is the real thing. Extreme steam action under the most dramatic and testing circumstances.

Hopefully the Tele Rail documentary programmes and this book go some way in illustrating our love of China and it's surviving steam operations. Quite simply, there is nowhere else on earth where working steam engines can still be seen in any serious numbers, other than China. But, of course, it's far more than quantity of operations – the harsh winters in the north, spectacular scenery, and wonderful light, can, if skilfully recorded, provide extraordinary photographs and spectacular video action. Despite the sheer physical distance from home, our passion for steam and a genuine affection for the Chinese countryside and rural way of life, has continued to grow.

All of our latter trips have been planned for the coldest winter months, when it can be a matter of life or death to have the correct heavy duty winter clothing. To enjoy the most spectacular steam effects it needs to be really cold – which is a strain not only on any one who has to stand around all day hoping that the temperature might creep up to minus 15° centigrade – but also for the camera kit. Modern electronic equipment with it's reliance on batteries can be particularly vulnerable, after all it's usually far colder than inside a domestic freezer! My rechargeable video batteries cope pretty well, but the small batteries used in the stills cameras often die with hardly any notice and constantly need checking.

The biggest problem is that if you're lucky enough to be able to get into somewhere warm at lunch time – the cameras will have to stay outside in the cold – otherwise they will quickly get covered in condensation which will freeze when you go back out after lunch. At the end of a typical day my camera and batteries lie on the hotel bed covered in frost just like a joint of meat from the freezer, and they usually take four or five hours to thaw out so that the batteries can be recharged.

Over the years we have accumulated our own favorite stories but I think, in retrospect, the silliest was the time that we were arrested for photographing a donkey! Although the Chinese authorities take a fairly positive attitude to rail fans, there are, of course, still strict rules concerning visits to certain parts of China. Some restricted areas, that were closed to overseas visitors, are only just now opening up – while most parts where working steam can be found, require some sort of alien's permit. Fortunately Li has always been able to relieve us of the official paper work for our visits. However, on one occasion a few years ago, things went wrong. Due to some particularly extreme weather at Jingpeng, we decided to leave early and spend an unscheduled day at the coal mines close to Chifeng. We realized that this was outside the area that was covered by our permit, but as we would technically be on 'private' property at the mine, we weren't unduly worried. Rather predictably for our unscheduled visit, the mine's management were on 'holiday' and we were refused permission to visit the site – so how should we spend what was left of the day?

Extreme winter conditions, throw into relief the efforts of a pair of QJs hauling a typical heavy freight. *JB*

As there were no really great line side spots, we opted to spend some time by a level crossing in the suburbs, and although there was little to see in the way of railway action, there was plenty of local life including a small street market with bicycles being repaired and plenty of people coming and going. I had been filming all the street activity when I noticed a man in a leather raincoat giving our local lady guide what appeared to be a very tough time. When we went to see what was happening he said that as we didn't have the correct paperwork we would all have to go to the local police station. The haul of a group of big noses created an immense amount of interest back behind the closed gates of the forbidding grey 1960s police building. Li and the local guide were summoned inside while we waited and waited in our mini bus. The only sign of life was windows occasionally opening to see the 'prisoners'. After an hour Li came out to say that the chief of police wanted our passports, so we knew things were starting to get a bit serious. Finally I was summonsed into the police station with my video camera – the official story was that a donkey man had complained that I had filmed him and his donkey cart without asking permission. In a grey room surrounded by Chinese officials I explained that under no circumstances would I wish to offend any Chinese person and dutifully rewound the tape and wiped the shots in question. Everyone then seemed happy enough, the chief of police saved face (essential in China), and some three hours after we were eventually allowed to go on our way.

In all our travels throughout China we've only occasionally bumped into other westerners, and with just one exception they've always been happy to share their knowledge of local locations and conditions with us. In the 1980s up-to-date information was hard to come by, but today thanks to the Internet, the China Rail page (http://severn.dmu.ac.uk) and the International Steam page (http://dialspace.dial.pipex.com/steam/internathtm) along with E mail, it's been possible to instantly keep in touch with many overseas friends and experts.

We've always made it our policy to stay in the best hotels that we could find – even so when you're traveling around some remote parts of Inner Mongolia the choice can be rather limited! The main problem is usually the lack of regular hot water – although there are some notable exceptions like the hotel at Reshui which is built over a thermal spring!

During the course of our travels we've enjoyed some excellent Chinese cuisine at a huge variety of establishments, from very basic country restaurants to expensive hotels. We've also occasionally sampled more unusual fare including hedgehog, snake, dog and exotic coloured fish but passed on the Chinese delicacy of whole chickens' heads and claws. Meals are normally accompanied by a bottle or two of the local pijiu or beer – most of which is more than acceptable.

One of the best times to enjoy a meal has always been while travelling by train between locations. Not only is the food usually pretty good – but it also helps to while away the hours on an interminable two or three day journey to some of the more remote areas. Of course, 'big noses' eating competently with chop sticks always attracts a good deal of attention, but none more so than in the restaurant car. With most of our expensive cameras and video kit needing to be carried around there's also the temptation to start working filming the chef and waiters. Being well fed the chances are that you'll sleep reasonably well – even when traveling overnight in third class sleeper – as we've had to do on the odd occasion. During one summer visit I remember being soaking wet and last onto the train in a monsoon. Needless to say my bunk was the top of the three, and right next to the loudspeaker which played interminable music for hours until the lights were promptly switched off by the dragon lady at 10 pm. As all the third class sleepers are completely open I had to try and sleep with the huge Betacam camera between my legs on the narrow bed. It wasn't so much that I was afraid that the expensive camera would be stolen – it was more a case of protecting the kit from the constant spitting from people in the other berths!

During our first visits there were still a few peasants to be seen wearing the old Chairman Mao boiler jackets – but nowadays even in the most remote areas that's a thing of the past. Most children and young factory girls in particular tend to dress quite fashionably. Although there is little change in the rural way of life, many thousands of workers have left the land lured to the cities by the comparatively high wages. Today Beijing is beginning to look more and more like any great cosmopolitan city – at the last count there were nearly forty branches of MacDonald's!.

No need for contrived photo run-pasts here trying to recreate the 'glory days' of the past – this is now, enjoy it while you can. *JB*

During our trips to China we have also got to know our fellow photographer and regular tour guide Li Weishu. Li had graduated from school in the top fifty from his province making him a real high flyer. Educated in China and the USA he is fluent in five languages and has also come to love the steam engines that crazy westerners want to see so much. An accomplished photographer himself, Li has been able to get us to every location we have ever asked to visit, and without him many of the pictures in this book would not have been possible. He's also helped me to carry our tripod with its massive – almost bazooka sized case – across so many stations that I've lost count!

We are very grateful to Li for adding a selection of his pictures to our collection and also to some other very accomplished photographers including Peter Skelton, Derek Short, Paul Stapleton, and Ted Talbot whose work also enhances this book.

As I'm always the 'man behind the video camera' it's been a particular treat for me to edit Extreme Steam. In this book regular viewers will recognise many of the locations from our Chinese documentary programmes, but in every instance that magical split second 'still' image has somehow captured the spirit of the moment – either it's action or the grandeur of working steam in the landscape. Rather than filling up page upon page with lengthy credits and details of the locations, we decided when first planning this book, that all the photos must speak for themselves, and for this reason we've tended to keep most credits as simple as possible throughout.

Michael, Vernon and I have done our best to ensure that Extreme Steam captures the magic of Chinese steam at the end of the 20th century. We are heading for China again soon and the anticipation is just as great as that first visit eight years ago. Thanks to the buoyant Chinese economy of recent years, many steam engines have been retained, to cope with the extra rail traffic. But, steam on the main lines is disappearing fast – every single day China Rail takes delivery of a new diesel. No one knows for certain, but from a peak of over 8000 steam locos the total figure is now less than 3000. Just like everywhere else, the steam engine is seen as a symbol of the past, and in 1999 China rail announced that main line steam would finish by October 1999. No one's certain of how the China Rail authorities define 'main line', and for the time being at least it looks like a fairly gradual decline of steam in the North.

There is however one ray of hope, currently there is still plenty of steam to be seen on the 'private lines' in China, where business is booming. At present a new route is being constructed off the Tongliao to Jining line to connect with the coal mine at Abagnar. The authorities confirm that the new route should open in 2003, and that it will be operated by double headed QJs on 2300 ton coal trains. However, things change fast in China, we have visited several locations to find steam had finished a few weeks earlier (although on one occasion it was reinstated again two months later!) Our advice, to anyone contemplating a visit, is as always, don't miss the greatest steam experience in the world – go now before it's too late!

Steve le Cheminant
Vernon Murphy
Michael Rhodes

At the end of the 20th century the sunset of Chinese steam was literally getting nearer by the day. *MR*

Throughout this book the following photographers are credited by their initials:

MR – Michael Rhodes
VM – Vernon Murphy
PS – Peter Skelton
PSt – Paul Stapleton
DS – Derek Short
JB – Julien Blanc
TT – Ted Talbot
LW – Li Weishu

Yebaishou

Yebaishou

Yebaishou is a small town of around 40,000 inhabitants, nestling in a river valley just over 200 kilometres North East of Beijing. Until 1995 it was out of bounds to foreigners, but then a relaxation in legislation allowed visits to begin. Three rail lines radiate from Yebaishou, west to Lingyuan and eventually Beijing, north to Chifeng and east to Fuxin and Shenyang. All the routes must climb out of Yebaishou, making the area an excellent setting to observe steam hard at work.

▲

The morning express from Chifeng breasts the summit at Shahai, 23 kilometres north of Yebaishou. Daybreak at the summit, with it's excellent inclines on both the north and south side, was always excellent with a steady procession of trains. *MR*

▶

The summit on the Chifeng line was host to a remarkable sight each morning as the first coal train of the day from the massive open-cast mine at Pingzhuang made it's way to Yebaishou. The motive power was always a pair of double headed QJs – yet despite the massive super steam power it would occasionally nearly stall on the final section to the summit. *PS*

◀ (preceding page)
Trains from Yebaishou, towards Lingyuan needed a banker for the first 10 kilometres of their journey. Heavy snow is comparatively rare here, but due to the extreme cold, an early sprinkling of snow was still on the ground in January 1996 as this pair of QJs, 2-10-2s toiled to the summit at Hongshi. *MR*

▲
Another freezing morning in January 1997 sees the Pinzhuang to Yebaishou
coal train round the corner just half a mile short of the summit at Shahai –
the sun has just risen moments earlier! *PS*

▲
As with most lines in China, freight services far out number the passenger workings. Only a couple of passenger trains travel from Yebaishou to Chifeng in daylight hours; the 14.37 departure, which was one of the last regular steam hauled main line passenger turns, makes swift progress up the hill to Shina. *VM*

▶
Inevitably in a country of over 1 billion inhabitants, some areas are quite densely populated with peasant farmers. Most Chinese refer to typical westerners as 'big noses' although by 1997, even the locals like this shepherd, were getting used to seeing the occasional rail fans who would descend on his valley for the day. *PSt*

▲
This view looking towards Yebaishou at the summit on the Lingyuan line was taken in January 1996. Just moments later a mad dash through knee deep snow, to the other side of the summit yielded the picture overleaf. There wasn't even long enough to photograph the QJ banker dropping off it's train at the feet of the photographers! *VM*

▶
The site of several brightly attired gentleman over six feet in height, rushing south over the summit to photograph the Lingyuan to Yebaishou trip freight was enjoyed by this rather henpecked chap. *DC*

◀
The line out of Yebaishou towards Shenyang is fairly level until it reaches Gongyingzi from where there is a steep winding ascent out of the river valley. In January 1996 a lengthy freight slows to walking pace a few yards short of the summit, before the easy descent to Bolouchi. *VM*

▲
In the Yebaishou area, only shorter local freight services like this morning trip from Lingyuan to Yebaishou yard, on the southern approaches to Hetanggou, were delegated to a single locomotive without bankers. *MR*

▶
A sunny day between Bolouchi and Gongyingzi found the team waiting for over an hour between trains. This kindly peasant was most concerned for our well being when he saw our thin outer Gortex trousers. It was not until we showed him the several layers beneath that he stopped insisting we retire to his hut for a cup of warming tea! *MR*

▶▶
Train 222, the lunchtime express from Yebaishou to Shenyang, winds uphill from Gongyingzi in January 1996. At this time, the service provided four hours uninterrupted steam haulage from Yebaishou to Fuxin, where diesel traction took over for the final leg to Shenyang. *MR*

▲

Dawn at Shahai summit was busy and train No.2181 rushes north with a pair of back to back QJs at the helm. Just minutes later the southbound coal from Pingzhuang was due in the other direction so the crew must reach the next passing loop quickly. The photographers have a similar dash to the other side of the summit to catch the coal on it's uphill slog. *MR*

▶

A train of coal empties from Yebaishou yard to Pingzhuang is light enough for a single QJ. Tender first workings, due originally to a lack of shed facilities, were always a common feature around Yebaishou, particularly on the Chifeng line. *VM*

▲
On another brilliant sunny day in January 1996,
a single QJ winds it's way further up the valley, past
Shina with the Pingzhuang empties. *MR*

▶
Around Shina the valley floor is so narrow that road
and rail are squeezed to within a couple of yards of
each other. More empty coal wagons are on their way
to the vast opencast mines around Pingzhuang. *VW*

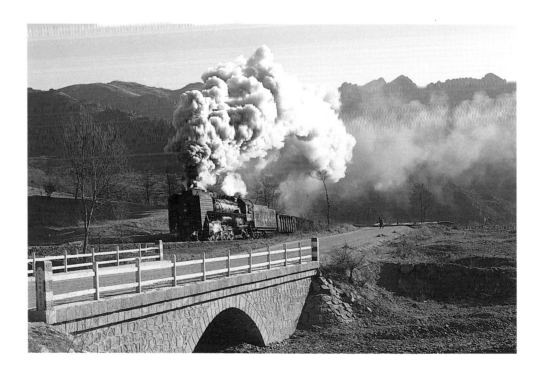

Last light in January in Yebaishou is around 16.00. Train No.2983 crosses the
frozen river just a mile out from Yebaishou as the last gleams of sun fade
away. An exposure of 125th second at f2.8 has just captured a scene which
would have been 'un-photable' only moments later. *MR*

▲
Many photographers spent their entire time in Yebaishou heading up to the hills, missing out on the frenetic activity around Yebaishou station itself. Train 453, the 14.37 departure from Yebaishou to Chifeng, starts on it's way north from Yebaishou. A tender first QJ waits to follow it up the hill with a freight, whilst a 2-8-2 JS busies itself shunting in the yard on the right. *MR*

▶
'Blow me down!' – dusk at Shina and steam turns to ice within moments when the ambient temperature is below minus 20°C. *MR*

▲
This could be the high veld but is infact between Shina and Shabai on the mainline from Yebaishou to Chifeng. Inspite of brilliant skies, the midday temperature never ventured above minus 10 during January of 1996. *MR*

▲
Even in such a vast landscape it's not always possible to keep out of
everyone's way. The figures of the Tele Rail video crew can just be seen in
the distance filming the action as the morning Pingzhuang to Yebaishou coal
train passes by toward the summit at less than walking pace – the sight and
sound were spectacular! *MR*

▲▶
Just west of Yebaishou station is the locomotive
depot. Fortunately for us all it was easily visible from
the main running line, which incidentally doubled up
as the main footpath out of town. Peter Skelton was
one of the few early visitors to get permission to visit
the extensive walled depot area, which at it's height
was responsible for over 50 locomotives. *PS*

▲▲▲

China Rail has an expanding network of over 50,000 kilometres. Although it has been trying to rationalise it's workforce, it still numbers into the millions with literally small armies of station personnel available to sweep snow from the platforms. Loco preparation is usually done out in the shed yard, which in the bitter winter weather often means literally hacking the ice from dripping cylinders with a hammer. *VM, MR*

▲▲

It's unusual to see women actually on the footplate – although they can often be found, along with other depot staff, cleaning out the ash pits at many sheds. Every carriage has a smartly dressed attendant or 'dragon lady' – but few are this young or pretty. *PSt, VM*

▶

Without an interpreter language is reduced to a few words of greeting, but it's amazing what a friendly smile and the offer of a cigarette will do! *PSt*

Chengde

▲
Wulie River skating rink forms the foreground for this 'Lowriesque' view of an afternoon coal train on it's way from Chengde to the steelworks. *VM*

▶
In the warm summer months a similar view of the Wulie River bridge is almost unrecognisable – even so a highly decorated SY class 2-8-2 makes a striking sight with it's morning coal train. *LW*

◀ preceding page
Four of the 21 steam locomotives owned by the Baiqi steelworks are caught in a single view at the banking station, in Chengde city. Twelve wagons, each with 60 tons of coal are as much as these three 2-8-2 locomotives can lug up the winding 1 in 33 incline. *MR*

Chengde

Chengde, 120 kilometres north of Beijing, is a thriving city which is famous as the seat of the emperor's summer palace. Steam predominated on the mainline until 1996, and remained the only motive power on the lengthy Baiqi steelworks branch to the north of the city. The steelworks are one of over 50 local steel plants across China, many of which have an internal rail network utilising steam traction.

The 30km line to the steelworks runs from the China Rail station, over the Wulie River, which freezes in winter and is used as a massive skating rink. The line then passes by city centre blocks of flats before a small yard marks the attachment point for bankers which propel the coal trains up a steep 1 in 33 incline. With as many as seven or eight trains running up the hill on a good day, the line has been a mecca for photographers for over 10 years.

▲
Sunrise at Chengde station – the morning rays have just illuminated the snow plough on the front of QJ 2678 as it struggles for it's footings on the way out of the goods yard en-route for Panjiadian. *MR*

▶
The JS yard pilot at Chengde – the dragon awakes! *MR*

▲
Chengde station at it's busiest, as the Longhua passenger departs north.
A JS fly-shunts, whilst an SY waits patiently in the yard for the passenger
to clear the junction for the steelworks branch. *MR*

▲ ▶
Six hundred tons of coal gathers speed as it is propelled away from the Chengde banking station by a trio of SY class 2-8-2 engines. The steelworks at Chengde owns 14 SY class engines, all built in Tangshan and also a further 7 of the more powerful JS 2-8-2 class, purchased second hand from China Rail. *Both VM*

▲
A JS leads the way out of the early morning smog over Chengde as the train heads for the steepest part of the climb and open countryside. *VM*

▶
Chickens for sale – and they don't come any fresher than this. *PSt*

▲
This is the more traditional angle for the steelworks branch. Invisible to the viewer is a small gallery of photographers – mostly from the UK and including one of our contributors Derek Short, who Michael had last met seven years earlier on the bridge at Severn Tunnel Junction in England – it's a small world *MR*

▶
Seconds later the haulers take centre stage, as they head for the tunnel that marks the summit. *VM*

Anshan Steelworks

Anshan steelworks is China's largest integrated
steel producing facility. It was built in 1906 by the
imperial Japanese and today covers 16 square
kilometres and contains 11 blast furnaces, 3 steel
making plants and 5 nearby iron ore mines.
A staff of 400,000 turn out 8 million tons of crude
iron every year. For us the interest lies in the internal
railway system, which employs a fleet of around 270
locomotives, nearly 70 of which are steam. These
three views give a flavour of the photographic
possibilities which this vast site offers.

▲
In the dank conditions of the steam shed, several SY class locomotives
undergo minor repairs. Since 1992, when this view was taken, the steam
fleet at Anshan has contracted somewhat. *MR*

▲
Fire and ice at Anshan, as molten slag is side tipped.
Even standing at the bottom of the tip in freezing
conditions the heat from the molten metal was
intense. The frozen 'waterfall' has been caused by a
burst pipe near to the loco which has to work
perilously close to the edge. *MR*

▶
A warm glow fills the air as molten iron is decanted
into waiting torpedos and cauldron wagons at
Anshan. The access to potentially dangerous areas,
with molten steel slopping out of torpedo wagons as
they are shunted around, is unlimited during these
works visits, and gives an excellent chance to catch
the gritty SY locos as they move around the huge
works. *MR*

Workshops

▲

Changchun is the last workshop to undertake rebuilds of China Rail steam locomotives. During our visit in 1998, there were locomotives from the Jitong line undergoing rebuilding as well as a new SY class engine being built for Hegang colliery railway in the north east. Deep in the gloom of the main workshop at Changchun QJ 7130 is being extensively rebuilt. *VM*

▶

By December 1998 the cavernous main shed at Changchun was a mere shadow of it's former self with just 1000 workers remaining where once there had been 3000. Predictions were that the shops would close within 2 years when work from the Ji-tong line runs out. *VM*

◄
Lanzhou workshops in the late 1980s were an amazing place with steam, diesel and electric traction for the entire China Rail network in the west of the country being maintained here. A QJ being re-tubed catches the morning sun. *DS*

▶
Two Ji-tong line QJs stand in Changchun. This remarkable 900 kilometre 'local railway' has a major shed in Daban which undertakes day to day repairs on it's fleet of QJs but all heavy overhauls are undertaken in Changchun, the last remaining work for this China Rail workshop. *VM*

▼
Like all major railway workshops the world over, Changchun boasts a scrap line! In December 1990, bits of QJs are scattered around the works as the locomotives are cut up for scrap metal. *MR*

Mundanjiang Area

Mundanjiang is a major Manchurian city with a population of 2.6 million. The mainline through the city is part of the route from Manzhouli to Vladivostock, built with the aid of the Russians and is a major freight artery. The engine sheds in Mundanjiang, Hengdaohezi, Muling and Jixi were all bastions of steam in the early 1990s. However, by January 1998 steam in the area was concentrated on just two sheds at Muling, which was 70% steam and Jixi which remained 100% steam.

▲

In 1997, there was still a heavy steam presence in Mundanjiang and the twice daily stopping service from Mundanjiang to Jixi and Mishan was nearly always QJ hauled. As daylight fades at 3pm in the far east of the country (the whole of China is on a single time zone), a QJ gathers speed for the climb round the loops at Modaoshi. *VM*

◄

The fireman has obviously been attending to his job as this pair of QJs leave Daqiaozi on the way from Muling to Mundanjiang. Ahead lies the steep climb to the lengthy loop around the small village at Modaoshi. Most crews get a small bonus based on the amount of coal burnt – and it's very unusual to see locos being over fired, belching black smoke, or blowing off unnecessarily. *JB*

▲

A typical day at Modaoshi in January 1998 yielded nine trains between
09.00 and 15.30. Five with steam haulage, but only three of these uphill,
two of which were passenger and this solitary uphill freight on it's way from
the hump yard in Mundanjiang to Suifenhe on the Russian border. *VM*

◄

The midday express from Mundanjiang to
Dongfanghong winds round the horseshoe at
Modaoshi in January 1998. The QJ will be exchanged
for another loxi based in Linkou at the half way
point on the journey to Dongfanghong, close to the
Russian border. *MR*

▲
Another view of the Dongfanghong express finds the train winding round the village of Da guan ling. Like so many scenes in this book, the ubiquitous DF4 diesel has taken over the passenger services from Mundanjiang. *VM*

▶
The evening passenger from Mundanjiang to Muling catches the last rays of winter sun. The timbers in the foreground protect precious mushroom patches which will blossom forth in the spring! *MR*

▲
Before the strict rationalisation of the China rail fleet of recent years, pairings like this high-deflectored JS 2-8-2 and a QJ 2-10-2 on the upper slopes of the Da guan ling loop on their way to the Russian border, were far more common. *DJ*

▲

The Jixi area contains 11 major mines where over 30 SY and JS locomotives help produce 20 million tons of coal each year. The largest single system of mines is at Hengshan about 12 miles south of Jixi. On the mining railway SY 1369 propels a spoil train along the dump track as the December light fades in 1998. *MR*

▶

As we entered 1999, Jixi shed retained an allocation of 16 QJs, several of which were highly decorated. Relegated from mainline passenger work to local colliery trips, No.3243 stands in the yard at Hengshan. *MR*

▲
Sunset at Hengshan. *MR*

◄
By December 1998, six DF4 diesels had arrived at Jixi – although they were nowhere in evidence at daybreak as four of the ??? ?? QJs were prepared for ??? to local collieries. *MR*

▲
The survival of steam for so long, even in reduced numbers, in remote areas
like Muling, meant photographers from all over the world were walking the
hills in the hope of finding a winning combination like this. *JB*

The Ji-tong line (Jinpeng pass)

The Ji-tong line was opened in 1996 and stretches over 900 kilometres from Jining to Tongliao. The first westerner to discover this new line was Julien Blanc from France and to him we owe a great debt of gratitude. The line is described as a 'local' railway. This designation signifies not it's geographical design but rather the source of it's funding which comes from 'local' government. In this case the

▲

The Ji-tong line has, so far, only ever seen regular steam haulage 24 hours a day. *JB*

◄
The Jinpeng pass is approached from the east via a massive double horseshoe formation. So within just a couple of hundred yards of hillside, there are three levels of track. Indeed they are so close that a fit photographer can actually catch the same train on each of the three levels! In January 1998 the air is remarkably still, and the usual driving wind has settled as two QJs tackle the second level above the town of Reshui. *MR*

▲
British outline semaphore signalling is a feature of the Ji-tong line and the brackets at the summit station are shown to good effect here. It could almost be Shap summit in the 1960s! *PS*

▲
The nail biting cold can almost be felt in this view taken just before dawn, where the ambient temperature on the summit may fall as low as minus 40° centigrade. This modern and well engineered line reaches a height of over 2,200 metres as it crosses the Jinpeng pass. *PS*

▲
A westbound freight at the second level line, just twenty minutes walk from Reshui and our small village hotel. *MR*

▶
Until 1999 the passenger service from Jining Nan to Tongliao ran only on alternate days because there was only a single set of carriages. This westbound train is just short of Jinpeng summit, which is one of the few spots that doesn't need a lengthy trek to get to, as it's right next to the main road and very easy to find. *MR*

▲
The main road from Galadesitai to Jinpeng crosses the railway at several points including this level crossing just one kilometre west of Reshui. This can tempt the photographer to chase trains which often can produce rather disappointing grab shots, and after several visits we found it better to either walk the line, or settle on a single location on the side of the pass with most uphill traffic for the day. Even so a bit of chasing can sometimes be fun! *VM*

►
Shangdian station at the summit of the Jinpeng pass seldom sees more than a handful of passengers. From above the station, an eastbound freight is on the final leg of the 25 kilometre climb from Jinpeng. *MR*

▲
Once again the Tele Rail video crew creep into the picture in their
environmentally friendly green jackets as a westbound freight enters the
tunnel just 500 yards short of Jinpeng summit. *MR*

◄
This eastbound freight really struggled to reach the
summit as the second locomotive had failed. The two
hour delay meant that two westbound freights were
waiting in the loops at the summit. The line is
operated so near to capacity that any locomotive
failure can have drastic knock on effects. *VM*

▲
In January 1998, a road journey from Siping to Reshui meant that we followed the Ji-tong line for much of it's length where we saw this westbound freight leaving Tianshan. Unbeknown to us this was a strictly 'forbidden' area, but we lived to tell the tale. *MR*

▶
The main locomotive depot for the Ji-tong line is located in Daban near the mid-point of the line. As well as a three track steaming shed to light locomotives up, protected from the bitter cold, there are two three track heavy lifting and maintenance sheds. The depot is responsible for between 40 and 50 QJ 2-10-2 locomotives and at the time of our visit in January 1998, there were 15 active locomotives on the depot as well as 6 dead engines. These included both new arrivals from China Rail as well as engines being cannibalised for spares. *MR*

▲▲
The western approaches to Jinpeng summit have many fine locations, but for some reason we have always found traffic very light in this direction. In January 1997 a pair of QJs approach the massive concrete viaduct, between Xiakengzi and the summit. *MR*

▲
The last rays of evening sun glint on a downhill freight heading east past Reshui. *LW*

▲
A westbound freight begins it's circumvention around the Reshui horseshoes. By the time the train passes in front of the photographer's feet, it will have travelled the best part of 10 kilometres. *VM*

Reshui village forms the backdrop for this shot of the westbound passenger service. One of the white blocks of flats is, in fact, a hotel which now caters for rail fans in the winter but was built to attract tourists to the local hot springs in the summer. It was only in 1997 that the hotel began to open during the winter months. *VM*

First light on the westbound approaches to Jinpeng summit. *VM*

For the more agile (like our Chinese colleague Li Weishu), there are some
spectacular vantage points on the western side of the pass. *LW*

▲
On a still morning in 1998, one of six westbound freights
nears the summit tunnel. *VM*

▶
Typical winter wear for many rural Chinese workers is this
heavy 'military style' coat which can be bought on most
markets for a few pounds. *PSt*

▲
In perfect winter light, an eastbound freight negotiates the spectacular
curved viaduct between Xiakengzi and the summit. *LW*

▶
Even coming downhill, the extreme cold and dramatic lighting can add up to a striking picture. *MR*

▼
The lengthy and spectacular horseshoe viaduct on the western side of the pass is seen to good effect in this low level view taken in January 1997. *MR*

▲
Departing from Xiakengzi, this eastbound train has another five kilometres or so
before it will pass over the horseshoe viaduct, in front of the photographer *VM*

▲
The Jitong line offers many good locations apart from the area either side of the Jinpeng pass. Between Tianshan and Xigou the main road passes over the line and we paused for a few moments whilst a westbound freight passed by. This train will have a second QJ attached at Daban for the trip through the Jinpeng pass to Haoluku. *MR*

▲ Inside the summit tunnel is a good place to shelter from the biting wind and also not a bad location to capture uphill trains. Moments later the photographer was engulfed in scorching steam and soot. *MR*

▶ What better advert for the magnificent scenery around the Jinpeng pass. *LW*

(Inset) High above Reshui is one of the 8-10 daily freights to be seen in daylight during January (on a good day!). *VM*

▲

In a 60 kilometers an hour gale at an ambient temperature of minus 30° centigrade, skin freezes very quickly. After a short sprint across the viaduct, as the train was already leaving Reshui station, Vernon quickly lost all sensation in his hands and face, and ended up with minor frostbite on his nose. *VM*

▶

By 1999 the frequency of passenger traffic had doubled to one train each day in both directions. The brightly decorated carriages are new rolling stock to cater for increased traffic. *LW*

First light east of Galdesitai, before the climb to the Jinpeng pass.
This westbound will pause in less than half a mile to allow a downhill
freight to pass. *MR*

▲
The sound and fury of this magnificent display was only equalled by the vitriolic outburst from one of our party who had discovered that his frozen fingers were not able to supply sufficient pressure to release the shutter to photograph this view just west of Reshui. *VM*

▶
Conditions in mountainous areas like this can change remarkably quickly, and even with the best winter clothes, hanging about in one location without walking to the next spot can be very unpleasant. *VM*

▲
One day in 1998 we elected to walk the 10 kilometres from the summit, back to Reshui. Just as we left Liudigou a howling gale blew up. Fortunately relief came when the station staff at Hudigou took pity on us, invited us in and supplied plenty of hot cups of tea. *VM*

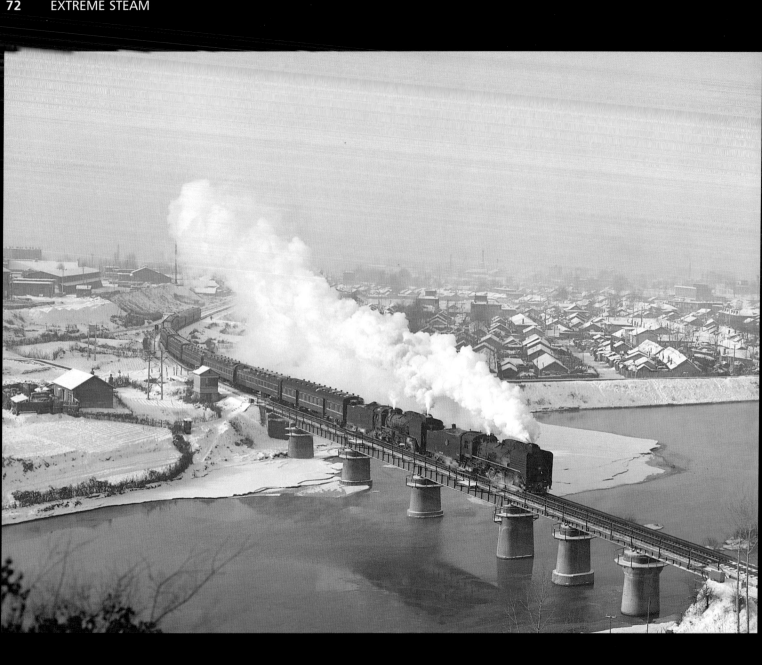

Tonghua & Tumen

Tonghua and Tumen are both sizeable cities with over a million inhabitants, near the North Korean border. They share another common theme in that both had sizeable fleets of JS 2-8-2 locomotives to work the steeply graded and tightly curved lines in the hilly area around the border.

▲

A pair of JS 2-8-2s 5141 & 5771 leave Hunjiang with the 06.13 Tonghua to Shuangyashan in January 1992. Traffic north of Hunjiang was restricted to JS class locomotives due to the tight curvature of the line. *PS*

A short freight from Hunjiang to Baihe makes a picture book scene just outside Hunjiang. *PS*

A little further up the line another single headed JS climbs over one of the dozens of small concrete bridges which characterize this steeply graded line from Tonhua to Hunjiang and Baihe. *DS*

▲
This QJ hauled freight from Wangquing to Tumen is drifting downhill towards the Xingxing spiral in January 1998. *MR*

▶
Both freight and passenger services on the branches from Chaoyangchuan were dealt with by JS 2-8-2s until mid 1998. In spring 1998 a Yanji to Helong passenger approaches Longjing. *LW*

▲
Freight traffic to the yard at Tonghua from the rest of China was QJ hauled and then remarshalled for forward movement behind JS locomotives. An express freight from the large marshalling yard at Meihekou is on it's way to Tonghua behind a pair of QJs. *JS*

▶
Tumenling, unlike it's name suggests, is nowhere near Tumen, but is situated between Changchun and Jilin. Passenger trains on this stretch were the last in China to use Pacific power. Towards the end of their reign, SL 644 works a Changchun to Jilin express. *DS*

Fuxin

A town of 700,000 people in the middle of a big mining area, Fuxin was out of bounds to foreigners until late in 1990. We understand from the local police and tourist board that we were the first westerners to be allowed into the China Rail roundhouse here. At the time of our visit in December 1998 the depot was home to 46 QJs, 7 JSs and 16 DF4 diesels. On top of that the local colliery railway serves 10 mines producing over 11 million tons of coal annually. It owns 30 SY 2-8-2 engines as well as 6 ex-China Rail QJs. Amongst it's services are sixteen daily passenger trains between Xinqui and Wangyang or Dongling via Fuxin.

▶

QJ 7116 in full passenger livery, retires to the shed after hauling the afternoon passenger turn from Jinzhou to Fuxin. The 1938 roundhouse at Fuxin was built by the Japanese and still has a dirt floor, and is likely to be demolished once the full quota of DF4 diesels on order arrive. *VM*

▲
During our visit in December 1998, the local mining administration were
keen to demonstrate what they might offer during a proposed 'steam festival'
and we were treated to this pair of SYs, painted up specially for our visit! *VM*

◄
Sujiatun, south of Shenyang was the priciple shed for
traffic on the Dalian mainline and was always busy
with a variety of motive power as this picture, taken
in 1996 shows. Sadly by 1999 this depot had been
completely dieselised *VM*

▲

Shenyang was until 1998, a busy steam centre. With two major yards in the city at Shenyang West and East, and two large yards out at Yuguo and Sujiatun there was plenty of inter-yard trip working. Both Shenyang West and East utilised British Dowty retarders although we were unable to ascertain whether these were licensed. In 1996 a deflector less JS leaves Shenyang West yard with a trip freight made of old refrigerator cars with frozen fish from Vladivostock to the local markets. *MR*

▶

The China Rail yard at Fuxin is a hive of activity with hourly departures to the east and to the west. On top of this two pilots busy themselves shunting and coal trains from the local colliery railway arrive throughout the day. A local railway employee takes water across the shunting neck at Fuxin *VM*

◀
A Fuxin to Yebaishou freight bursts out of the morning smog in Fuxin during a particularly cold snap in December 1998. *MR*

▼
Passenger services between Fuxin and Jinzhou remained in the hands of the mighty QJs until well into 1999. The morning train to Jinzhou crosses a viaduct between Yamatu and Aiyouying. *VM*

▲

First light and our group were concentrating on the colliery railway, just yards behind the photographer, when this QJ burst into sight on the converging main line from Yebaishou to Fuxin. *MR*

▶

This battered old QJ, with it's smoke deflectors removed, looks distinctly different, and has been relegated to the yard pilot at Fuxin. Probably no more than another year of life remains for this ageing dinosaur. *VM*

▲
The only active catholic cathedral in China (we were told) is just outside Fuxin and forms the backdrop for this picture of the afternoon Jinzhou to Fuxin express. QJ 7118 is just 5 kilometres from it's home base in Fuxin and will be on the shed within the hour. *MR*

Pacifics – gone but not forgotten

One aspect of the China Rail scene which has long
gone is mainline working by the RM and SL
pacific engines – but thanks to Derek Short, the
Pacifics will not be forgotten.

The SL pacifics were known as the 'Victory' type and were first built as long
ago as 1933. Production of the class of over 400 locos ceased in 1958. In
March 1989 SL 627 works through the outskirts of Jilin with a Changchun
express. *DS*

The passengers on this Dalian - Anshan express, are only able to glimpse
the interesting scenery around the famous Porcupine Hill, as they are
whisked past by SL 631. *DS*

The pacific RM class was the successor to the SL, and included a new Russian designed boiler on the same chassis as the SL. The RMs were considered to be particularly suitable for express and long distance passenger work, and could often be seen racing to Changchun. *DS*

▲
By 1994, China Rail had doubled the route from Shapatou to Changliushui but the motive power was still dominated by steam. Uphill and downhill traffic meet near Sisuo. *PS*

Zhongwei

For many of us, our first introduction to Chinese steam came deep in the Gobi desert, west of Zhongwei at the inland end of the Great Wall. Here a ten kilometre climb through several horse-shoe curves provided the chance to watch steam at it's finest. Sadly the line west from Zhongwei has been electrified for some time and the massive steam shed at Zhongwei, once home to over 70 QJ 2-10-2 engines, lies silent and steamless. This shorter sevice a reminder of the glories of desert railroading at it's finest.

◀

Kilometre 722 – one of the ten great railway locations in the world! As well as a steady procession of double headed trains, most days saw also an afternoon triple headed express freight – although being in the right place at the right time often proved to be somewhat of a challenge. *PS*

▲
High above the mighty Yellow River, with it's gleaming riverside mosque, army vehicles are hauled west by a pair of beautifully decorated QJs. Taken in August 1994, this was the final year for steam from Zhongwei. *JB*

▶
The Beijing to Lanzhou express, or Train 44 as it was known, was steam hauled from Datong west – over 2000 kilometres behind steam. The famous train is on the last portion of it's long journey approaching Mengjiawan. *VM*

▲
When splendid views like this at kilometre 722 in January 1997 first
appeared in 'Steam Railway', it quickly became obvious that a visit to China
would be well worth while. Little did we know then that every subsequent
year would see us drawn back once again to find more steam action. *PS*

▲
Further west in the Pingkoaxia gorge, the mountain scenery becomes more rugged. During the early 1990s steam was responsible for nearly all traffic west from Zhongwei to Lanzhou and Wuwei, but between 1992 and 1995 literally hundreds of QJs were withdrawn as both diesel and electric traction displaced these mighty engines, many to the scrap line. *PS*

▲▶
In October 1992, the weather was perhaps
a little too warm for true 'extreme steam'
but in shirt sleeves and with bottle of beer
in hand freight after freight passed the hill
at kilometre 722. As the day wore on the
harsh desert light became more stark and
temperatures rose from around freezing at
dawn to nearly 20° centigrade. MR

▲

As well as general goods traffic, the line through
Zhongwei carried a large amount of oil from the oil
fields in the far west around Wulumqi. Last shot of
the day near Mengjiawan finds this typical trainload
outward bound. *PS*

▶

A large new freight yard was eventually built at
Shapatou, however in 1994 freight traffic still passed
through Shapatou on it's way to the cramped sidings
adjacent to Zhongwei station. *VM*

▶

Part of the appeal of China is that this is very much an everyday working steam railway – just as it used to be decades ago in every other country. It's not always the dramatic action that rekindles happy memories, sometimes it's a faraway whistle at night, or perhaps like this just a glimpse of a distant train across a frozen river at Mengjiawan. *PS*

▼

A little further north of Zhongwei the scenic branch line from Pingluo to Rujigou tended to get far fewer visits from photoghraphers, which was a shame as the route had some stunning locations *PS*

▲
Floods and drought in the Gobi desert have combined over hundreds of years to chisel these mounds of earth in the valley of a dried up river. One of ten uphill freights on this particular day in 1992 winds past Sisuo. *MR*

▶
Train 44 pauses at Linhe to take water before continuing west to Zhongwei. Over the years scenes like this have become steadily rarer as most sheds got their first allocation of diesels, and the remaining QJs were downgraded from 'top link' duties. *VM*

◀
Chinese steam crews are well known for their outstanding abilities to keep heavy trains on the move without burning prodigious amounts of coal. It's rare to see an engine really being thrashed and steady regular progress is the normal order of the day. Even so the extra resistance from the curves just beyond Shapatou yard caused this pair to loose their feet for a few seconds before the driver regained control. *VM*

▲
For many people Zhongwei became the 'greatest show on earth', and over
the years rail fans from all over the world came to witness this superb
spectacle. Those who were privileged to visit Zhongwei, have so much to be
grateful for. *MR*

Narrow Gauge

Narrow Gauge

Despite recent closures there are still plenty of narrow gauge systems around China. The most common gauge is 762 mm and the ubiquitous P45 0-8-0, whose origins are in Poland and Russia, can be found at work in mines, collieries, and most of all on forestry railways. With comparatively small trains hauling huge loads, the narrow gauge lacks none of the drama of the standard gauge, and often being situated in the more remote areas usually has the additional benefit of plenty of extra charm.

◀

The Hunjiang ironstone railway was perched high above Hunjiang and employed over a dozen C2 class engines. *MR*

▼

Yabuli shed comes to life in December 1998. This was probably the last season for this forestry line as there are now strong ecological pressures on the forestry authorities to stop extracting timber from the forests to the north. *VM*

◀ (Preceding page)
Xilin mineral railway employs five 0-8-0 engines to ferry lead 20 kilometres from a mine to a smelting plant in Xilin. The yard pilot splutters into action in January 1998 on a morning where the minus 30° centigrade temperature is almost visible. *MR*

▲
The most atmospheric time to visit Hunjiang depot was usually in the early evening as crews returned to base before dusk. *MR*

▶
Xilin yard and the pilot potters around in the early dawn, ready to marshal the first trainload of empties bound for the mine. *VM*

▲
Weihe, only an hour or so from Yabuli, is fortunate in having retained, for the time being at least, it's steam hauled passenger service to Liu-shan. Despite competition from the local bus service there were still plenty of passengers to be picked up at Xing Li in January 1999. *TT*

▶
This far north, logging doesn't normally start well into December when the ground will be frozen hard enough to make felling operations easier. So we were particularly fortunate to catch the first train of the season leaving Yabuli in early December 1998, loaded with empties and several van loads of supplies for the harsh winter season out in the forests. *MR*

▲

If the end of the 1999 logging season does indeed see the complete closure
of this once extensive narrow gauge system, the implications for the town of
Yabuli could be quite dramatic. Many people rely on the railway's rail buses
for transport, and have jobs in some way connected with logging. *VM*

▲
Conditions this far north east in China can be really
harsh in winter, with extreme cold and very short
days with sunset around 15.00. *MR*

▶
There are two narrow gauge systems within striking
distance of the Chinese capital, one at Yexi and the
other, here at Dahuichang. Over recent years many
railfans have visited these lines on their first or last
day in Beijing while filling in time before flying home.
It's certainly good to know that entering the new
millennium there is still steam within an hours drive
of the centre of Beijing! *TT*

▲
The truncated Weihe system once served many more logging points, but has
been greatly rationalised in recent years. Despite it's closeness to Yabuli it
was unknown to western railfans until 1999. Three kilometres out from
Weihe, a train of empty wagons gathers speed behind China's narrow gauge
workhorse, the C2. *TT*

▲
Old and new on Yabuli shed. The remaining active 0-8-0s are steamed for what may well be the last season and by the end of the year they will probably join their compatriots in the scrap line. *MR*

▶
Many local farmers around Yabuli continue to use donkeys as their main beasts of burden. Without exception all the animals were well fed and seemed to cope with the slippery conditions underfoot remarkably well. *VM*

Fifty kilometres north of Beian is the Zhanhe forestry railway, which runs east for over 130 kilometres into some very remote forest areas. Unlike the shorter logs, which are more commonly seen at Yabuli and Weihe, a large proportion of the timber from Zhanhe is transported as complete tree trunks which are strapped to bogies at either end, with the huge tree trunks taking the tractive forces. *TT*

▲

After stopping for a blow up a single C2 with five gondolas of frozen lead ore tackles the lower slopes, before the steep final incline to Xilin. In spite of an ambient temperature of minus 20° centigrade, several Chinese ride the train, unprotected from the elements. The ore must be placed in a warming shed at Xilin before it can be removed from the wagons where it has frozen solid. *VM*

▶

Although this yard pilot was on hand for shunting in the main reception sidings at Yabuli, some of the wagons, including the guards van, are light enough to be easily pushed clear of the points by hand. *VM*

Nancha & the Far North

By the last decade of the 20th Century, nearly half of all operational steam locomotives were based in the north of China. This is an area with a dense railway network that owes much to Japanese and Russian invaders. The climate with frequent brilliant blue skies and biting cold in winter makes the far north of China a photographer's paradise.

▲
Nancha bank is a short sharp climb out of Nancha on the line north to Wuyiling. All but the lightest of trains are assisted up this section and it has been the location for some of the most enduring images of Chinese steam. *PS*

▶
Much of the traffic south into Nancha from Wuyiling and Yichuan was timber from the endless birch forests, which stretched north to the Russian border. Sadly poor planning has led to severe deforestation and in 1998, there was unemployment reaching 50% around Yichuan due to loss of jobs in the logging industry. In happier times the Yichuan timber approaches Nancha from the north. *PS*

▲
After a brisk start the Wuyiling passenger braves the incline out of Nancha without assistance, it's only a few kilometres to the summit where speed will gradually fall to little more than a walking pace. *PS*

▶
Even in 1996, most of the freight traffic on the mainline to Jiamusi was still steam as well as all the trains on the branch to Yichuan. Although less photographed the mainline was busy with both freight and passenger trains. *PS*

▲
Much of the timber was initially collected by a
multitude of narrow gauge lines far to the north,
before being transferred to standard gauge wagons
for the last part of the journey south to Nancha.
These heavy trains nearly always needed three QJs
to help them slowly over the long slog to the final
summit before the steep descent into Nancha. *DS*

▶
With most people in the suburbs cooking on fires
powered by coal brickets, pollution is often a
problem in even the smaller Chinese towns like
Nancha. The sun struggles to break through the
smog here, although there is clear sky just a few
kilometres away on the incline out of Nancha. *JB*

▲

Stepping crisply east along the mainline to Jiamusi, this highly decorated QJ with it's enthusiastic driver make a great sight. *PS*

▶

It's not only film crews that have to struggle with a heavy load! *PSt*

▲
An optimistic sunrise near Nancha and the promise of
another day of unrivalled steam action means it was
certainly worth missing breakfast at the hotel. *PS*

Speeds on the mainline often reached 70 kilometres per hour, and this pair of QJs are certainly not hanging around on their way from Nancha to Jiamusi. *PS*

▲
Jiamusi itself was a real steam mecca, and even in 1999 the shed still had 20
QJ locomotives for working freight to Boli. Back in January 1998, a single QJ
drifts across the Jiang River on the approach to Jiamusi from Nancha just

▲

A pair of QJs cross the viaduct at Aobaogo, just south of Dongsheng. The coalfields to the south currently produce 10 million tons of coal a year, much of which is loaded onto rail at twelve points along the mainline to Shenmu. The projection is for the coalfield to produce 60 million tons of coal each year by 2005. Due to the immense economic implications of this huge coal reserve, the line is currently being electrified, and a new cut off is being built to allow direct access to Datong (avoiding Baotou) and hence to the massive coal export facility at Qinhuangdao. Work is due to be completed by 2002 so go now before it's too late! *MR*

Baotou

Baotou, the largest city in the autonomous region of Inner Mongolia, had everything for the steam enthusiast. A massive steel works which at it's peak boasted a fleet of over 60 steam engines, local branch lines with steam haulage, a suburban passenger network, again steam operated and a busy mainline, which until 1995 was also predominantly steam run. Add to all this a brand new line to the coal mines in the south around Shenmu which only opened in 1996 and Baotou should be on anybodies list when they visit China for steam.

◀

Steam still flourishes in 1999 in Beian, far to the north of Harbin, where a small fleet of high deflectored JS 2-8-2s handle local freight – for the time being at least. *TT*

◄

The line from Baotou to Dongsheng and Shemnu is a local railway, funded by the local government and the mining administration. It has purchased a fleet of 22 QJ engines from China Rail, and built the line with modern concrete sleepers and colour light signalling - but points are still manual! *VM*

►

This single QJ struggling along, 3 kilometres south of Aobaogo can look forward to gradients of up to 1 in 80. *VM*

▼

Traffic patterns vary enormously on the Dongsheng line, but on this day we were treated to eight uphill trains between 08.00 and 15.30. The first train of the day at Aobaogo produced a single QJ with nearly 2000 tons of coal in tow. *MR*

▲

A banking engine is based at Dongsheng yard and may be called for loads deemed too heavy to tackle the climb through Aobaogo alone. On this occasion the train had just exceeded the 2000 tons a single QJ could manage and the banker was attached. *MR*

▶

During a busy day most trains must wait in Aobaogo station for southbound traffic to pass. *MR*

▲

Between Baotou and Dongsheng are the 'Singing Sands', a Chinese tourist attraction, named after the sound the wind makes as it whistles past. There's even a chair lift to allow sand skiing down the dunes! Much more of an attraction is the lengthy concrete viaduct crossing the junction between the desert and scrub and the heavy coal traffic which continually passes over it. *MR*

▶

The Shiguai branch once served many local mines most of which were worked by local peasants on a very small scale. Until 1999, the line was worked by JS 2-8-2 engines based at Baotou Dong. Today there are abandoned drift mines all around here although a few still produce enough coal for local needs. Corn for winter (stored on the roof of the house), is often seen in small villages, all over this part of China. *MR*

▲

The exhaust from QJ 6289 has almost obscured the cooling towers of a massive, modern, coal fired power station. The juxtaposition of modern concrete structures alongside traditional steam traction seems somehow rather incongruous. *VM*

▶

The Singing Sands have encroached beyond the protective layer of trees where it's quickly blown into new shapes. With 24 hour action more coal empties head south to Dongsheng in December 1998. *VM*

▲
Undoubtedly the 'train of the day' is the mid-morning coal train which regularly loads to 3300 tons and needs three QJs to reach the summit at Dongsheng. Having decided that this viaduct just north of Aobaoqo offered the best viewpoint for the lengthy train, it proved to be rather more difficult than we originally anticipated to get a good shot. Only, after two previous attempts, frustrated by swirling wind, was the train finally caught with the smoke blowing away from the camera. *MR*

▲▲

When morning temperatures in December can be as low as minus 20° centigrade, even downhill traffic can provide reasonable steam effects. A long rake of empty coal wagons winds over the viaduct, just south of Aobaogo station. *MR*

▲▶

An extensive locomotive depot has been built to service the line and is located in Dongsheng. Visitors are welcome for a small fee and the fleet of 22 QJs can be photographed at leisure as they are coaled, steamed and repaired. *Both MR*

▲▲
From the driver's point of view it's all downhill with a heavily loaded coal train past Singing Sands. The curious geological features here and the shifting sand meant this huge viaduct had to be built close to the sandstone cliff. *MR*

▲
The sprawling steelworks at Baotou are glimpsed on the horizon as a single QJ heads for Bayan Obo. *VM*

▲

Rush hour at Baotou Dong and JS 8001, leaves the station with a typical
suburban passenger service. During a one hour observation period at the
station throat in 1998, we witnessed steam departures to Linhe and on the
suburban loop service, as well as eight freight trains with DF4 diesels and
two passenger workings which were diesel hauled. In addition there were
shunting movements from the nearby yard and locomotive depot. *VM*

▶

Hohot depot, to the east of Baotou also retained an allocation of JSs. The
class were built as the successor to the standard JF type and once numbered
over 1000 locos. *VM*

Baotou steelworks has very few pollution controls! The complex still boasts some unusual steam motive power and one of the works YJ 2-6-2 engines moves alongside one of the new diesels. *PS*

Most Chinese steam sheds were organised to follow the American practise of disposal and preparation. In 1994 Baotou Xi depot was a wonderfully atmospheric place still busy with all the everyday activities associated with steam. VM

▲
The ET7 0-8-0 tank is a non-standard class found in Baotou steelworks where these little engines can still be seen shuttling under the blast furnaces. *PS*

▶
The line to Bayan Obo winds through the hills north of Baotou for 150 kilometres. Built solely to transport iron ore to the steelworks in Baotou, recently the route has finally been fully electrified, and the sight of a QJ here is just a memory. *VM*

▲▲
It's doubtful if any of the passengers on this Shiguai to Baotou service that's approaching Houba realise that the JS that is working this service will soon be scrap. *VM*

▲
A typical line up of 'big noses' and local guides enjoying a break between the action. Left to right, two local guides, Li Weshu, Bob Avery, Steve le Cheminant, Bob Powell, and Vernon Murphy. *MR*

▲
In some countries the local urchins can be quite a problem, but most Chinese children, unlike this small group at Jiamusi, tend to be initially at least, rather wary of big noses – although nearly all of them enjoy shouting 'hello' in a rather mocking tone. *PSt*

The Culprits

Vernon & Steve 'enjoy' a typical rail fan's lunch of instant noodles. *MR*

Although it was only just after dawn, and this small restaurant on the road to Reshui was closed, Li was able to persuade the owner to quickly rustle up a superb breakfast of pancakes. *LW*

Communications with home initially meant frustrating delays while disinterested hotel receptionists attempted to get an international line. Then a few years ago it first became possible for Michael to phone home with Li's mobile from the top of the hill at Reshui, and last year we could use our own mobile phones for the first time! *LW*

This is more like it, as the duty free bottle of Vosne Romanay is finally enjoyed before retiring for the night on the Beijing to Baotou sleeper. *LW*

It doesn't get any more luxurious than this in the 'outback'. Welcome to the 'Yabuli Hilton' complete with (for the more lucky) huge radiators mounted just above the bath! *MR*

The coldest day of our lives; minus 30° centigrade, plus a continuous 50 kph wind that made photography so difficult that we all had to retire early to the comparative warmth of our hotel. *MR*